Last, First,
Middle
and Nick

Last, First, Middle and Nick

All About Names

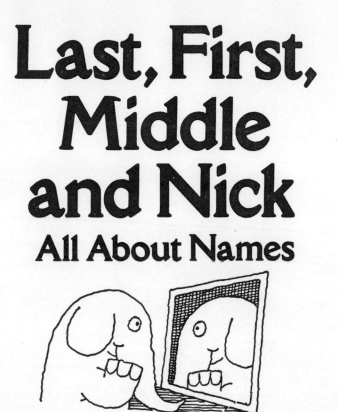

by Barbara Shook Hazen

Illustrated by Sam Weissman

Prentice-Hall, Inc. Englewood Cliffs, New Jersey

Printed in the United States of America   J

Prentice-Hall International, Inc., London
Prentice-Hall of Australia, Pty. Ltd., North Sydney
Prentice-Hall of Canada, Ltd., Toronto
Prentice-Hall of India Private Ltd., New Delhi
Prentice-Hall of Japan, Inc., Tokyo
Prentice-Hall of Southeast Asia Pte. Ltd., Singapore
Whitehall Books Limited, Wellington, New Zealand

1 2 3 4 5 6 7 8 9 10

For Brack, his Shook cousins
and all the Evanses.

Contents

Chapter One
What's My Name to Me

Your name is the most important word you will ever hear.

It identifies you as **you**. It's your label—on school books and addresses, on your passport and other important papers.

It's the word friends and family call when someone wants you to come to dinner or play ball or greets you on the street. It's the word picture that brings you instantly to mind, even when you are not there.

Shakespeare said a rose by any other name would smell as sweet. This may be true of roses. Flowers don't have feelings. People do.

How you feel about your name has a lot to do with how you feel about yourself. Likely, if you like your name, you like being yourself. If you can't stand your name, or feel it doesn't fit the skin you're in, it's harder to like who you are.

Your name affects the way others react to you. In a "blind" psychological study, schoolchildren were asked to grade papers written by classmates. The papers were all equal in merit. The names put on the papers were a made-up mixture of popular and unpopular first names.

The schoolchildren doing the grading gave the papers with the most popular names, such as Lisa and David, the best grades. Papers with Prudence and Humboldt on the top did not fare so well.

What does this mean? That your teacher will give you a failing grade if your name happens to be Prudence or Humboldt? Or that classmates will snub you?

Not at all. It merely means that the instant reaction to your name may not be quite as favorable. All else being equal, a David on an after-school job application may have an edge over a Humboldt.

But all else usually isn't equal. When Humboldt (or Prudence) appears in person for a job interview, he may well have the edge. Because strong, different names tend to develop people who have strong, individualistic personalities. Also they are less likely to get lost in the shuffle.

2

What really matters is how you feel about your name. Lyndon Johnson was always proud of his unusual name, even as a child. So was Hubert Humphrey. He named his son Hubert, too. As a girl named Courtnay put it, "Who **wants** to have a name like everyone else. My name makes me feel special."

Whether it is one of the hundred most popular or one-of-a-kind, your name should make you feel special. It should make you feel good inside when you hear it or see it or write it.

If not, you may want to change it. But first, the more you know about your name, and names in general, the better equipped you will be to decide.

Learning about names is a good way of getting better acquainted, with yourself and with your friends. It is also an interesting way of discovering things about your roots and ancestors. And it is fun!

As Humpty-Dumpty said, "My name means the shape I'm in." Think a bit as to how your name has shaped **you**.

It's Not My Name But the Way You Say It

One day in September a man from a charitable organization took a poor fatherless boy to a store to buy him some school clothes. When the man asked to see a suit for the boy, the salesperson sized up the situation and brought out the cheapest suit he had. The boy slumped. His face fell.

The man spoke up indignantly, "Don't you recognize this boy. This is John Adamson. I want you to bring out your **best** suit."

The boy perked up. He had never before heard his name spoken so proudly. From then on, he was never the same. He lived up to his best, what he heard in the way the man said his name.

A Few Psychological Facts

Name calling is second to assault as a cause of murder.

Crazy people tend to forget their real names and make up new ones. Sometimes they think they are someone else, like God or the devil.

One of the most brutal punishments for a prisoner is to have his name taken away and to be called by a number.

Putting your name on your work increases productivity. A big paper company was turning out too large a percentage of faulty paper bags. When each machine operator was asked to put his name on the bags he made instead of a number, the reject percentage dropped from 6 to 1.

People who use your name a lot probably like you a lot.

THAT'S _MY_ BAG!

BAG MADE BY Fred

Chapter Two
Remembering Names and How to Be Better at It

Former Post Master James A. Farley claimed to have a memory bank of over 50,000 names. Napoleon claimed he could recall the names of all his subordinates.

On the other hand, Teddy Roosevelt once stretched out his hand to a well-wisher who said, "Remember me? I made your shirts."

"Ah, yes," Teddy Roosevelt replied. "Major Shurts. I'd know you anyplace."

Everybody loves to have his or her name remembered. Most of the time most of us aren't as good at it as we'd like to be. We simply forget—the name of the boy we played with and liked, the name of the girl we had a good time with in the park.

Other times, psychiatrists suggest, we may "forget" on purpose. We may subconsciously forget the name of someone we don't like or want to remember, or who makes us anxious.

But most of the time we **do** want to remember. Are there any tricks to remembering better?

One is to repeat the name as often as possible after you meet the person. Using the name is friendly, and it helps engrave it on your memory.

If you're not sure of the spelling or pronunciation, ask to have the name repeated. It shows interest. And we all like people who are interested in us.

There's nothing wrong in admitting that you have a lousy memory. Many people do, and it works better than pretending to remember.

Word association is another memory trick. If you meet a boy named Humphrey Winter, you might mentally picture a humpless camel trudging along in the snow.

But word associations can backfire. A girl named Virginia Stockfish was once greeted as Alabama Fishstew, and another girl named Hazel was told, "I don't exactly remember your name, but I know you're some kind of nut."

Name Sayings

Big name personality: Worthy of being on a magazine cover.

Name your price: What's the least you will take for it.

That's the name of the game: That's the gist of the business, the meat of the matter.

To say someone's name is mud: To dismiss him or her as unworthy.

Nameless entity: A total zero.

You can't eat it if you name it: You can't hurt what you've grown fond enough of to name, as the calf you raised yourself, the chicken you call Biddy, who is a pet.

Make a name for yourself: What everybody wants— to have a name that is instantly recognized, well thought of, and respected.

Name Words

Many words in common usage come from proper names. Here are a few.

Pullman, Bunsen burner, silhouette, and **daguerreotype,** from the last names of the men who invented them.

Mesmerize (which means to put into a trance), from Anton Mesmer, who claimed to "cure" patients by means of a special magnetic fluid that flowed from him to them.

Dextrous (which means right-handed and/or skilled with the hands), from the Latin name Dexter.

Courteous, from the French name Curtis.

Zinnia, from the Professor named Zinn.

Poinsettia, from the ambassador of the same name. (Flowers are commonly named after people.)

Sandwich, from the Earl of Sandwich, who invented a handy way of eating.

Sadist (a person who is mean to others), from the Marquis de Sade, who was.

STOP THAT, MARQUIS! YOU'RE SURE GOING TO GROW UP TO BE A SADIST, YOUR HIGHNESS!

Name Names

Given Names: The legally registered first and middle names given you at birth.

Surname: Your last name, the one inherited from your father.

Family Name: Another name for surname.

Maiden Name: The last name a woman was born with, as opposed to her married name.

Nickname: The shorter, friendlier name based on your real name or picked up on the playground.

Pseudonym: A fictitious name, generally used by an author to conceal the real name.

Pen Name: A made-up name used by authors.

Stage Name: The made-up name of a stage or screen or singing star.

Sobriquet: Old-fashioned word for nickname, sometimes used for stage name.

Handle: A nickname for name, often used to identify CB radio owners.

Alias: An assumed name for criminal (or other) concealment.

Code Name: Short disguised name used by spies and government officials.

Onomastics: The study of the origin and history of names.

Chapter Three
Given Names, How You Got Yours

You have many choices in life. What you are legally named is not one of them. What you are called is.

All babies are registered at birth. But not all babies are registered with their given names. Sometimes they are called "Boy Randall" or "Girl Jones" till the parents make up their minds.

President Johnson didn't have a legal given name for months after he was born. His parents simply couldn't decide.

One morning, mother Rebekah Johnson refused to fix breakfast until there was a final decision. Father Sam Johnson suggested the name of his brother-in-law Clarence.

Mrs. Johnson vetoed that saying that as Clarence had always hated his own name why saddle anyone else with it. Neither one wanted a junior.

Finally, after a long "no" list, Linden was suggested. It was the name of a close friend of Sam's. Mrs. Johnson said fine, but only if she could spell it differently.

"Spell it anyway you please," said Sam. "He will still be my friend." And so, Lyndon was chosen.

One child was given over a dozen first names when the minister at the christening read the wrong side of a piece of paper—the one listing all the possible names rather than the one that was finally decided upon.

Screenwriter Frank Stanley Gilman Gordon Chase was given his string of names in the hopes that someday the rich relatives he was named for would remember him. They didn't, and later he legally snipped his name down to Gordon Chase.

Sometimes circumstances dictate the choice. Twins born at flood crest were named Highwater and Overflow. A serious beer drinker named his three sons Budweiser, Falstaff and Michelob. A writer named her daughter Olivetti.

The special circumstances can be political. I had a great-aunt named Union Forever Shook. She was born during the Civil War and her parents wanted to protest the fact that some members of the family turned rebel. She was called Una, which wasn't so bad. Neither is Missy, whose real name was Missouri Compromise. More recently, in California, a baby girl was named Equal Rights Amendment. Perhaps she will end up Equa.

In Ceylon—and less often elsewhere—the choice of names is governed by the stars. Places are another source. Actors James and Pamela Mason named their daughter Portland after their favorite city.

A baby may be named for something that happens near the time of birth. One mother named her daughter Angel after hearing the Angelus bells. Zelda Fitzgerald was named after a gypsy queen in a novel her mother was reading at the time. So was my Aunt Amber Jean, who tried to keep her real first name a family secret and used her middle name. Many babies are named after the most popular personalities of the day.

There are always a few oddball names, like Seven Eights and Wowie. There are always a few product names, like Catsup and Vaseline.

By far the largest number of babies born are named after someone in the family. Or two someones.

The first name may be taken from one side of the family; the middle name from the other. Occasionally the first name itself is a fusion of both parents names. Child preacher Marjo Gortner's first name combined Mary and Joseph.

But the majority of names are chosen simply because the parents like them. They like the sound and the feel of the name. It may be that one parent would have liked to have been called that himself, or liked someone with the name. And the largest number of these are the names that have come down through the ages—the names found in the baby naming books, which become the names found in history books.

Juniors

Giving the son the same first name as the father is an Anglo-Saxon custom. John Adams has a son, who is John Adams, junior. He may be called Junior or Chip (for chip off the old block) or Tad (for tadpole off the old frog) or Sonny to eliminate confusion. He may also be called Jack or by his middle name.

Generally Jewish parents do not name a child after the father, or any living relative. Long ago the prophet Judah warned that a man's soul might be deprived of rest after death if his name was given to another during his lifetime.

In Arab countries, there is no form for a junior. If you are named after your father, the entire name must be repeated. Thus the full name of a UN delegate was Ibrahim Allam Ibrahim Allam.

Some psychologists think that it may be harder for a child named after his father to develop and assert his own personality. Which depends, in fact, more on the individual relationship than on the name.

Chapter Four
A Mini History of Naming

God named the first man Adam. No one is sure when man began naming his fellow man.

En-lil-ti, which most scholars think is a human name, appeared on an Egyptian tablet as far back as 3300 B.C. Several centuries later, about 5,000 years ago, an Egyptian pharoah was named N'Armer.

The earliest names were descriptive. They identified their owners as short or tall, blonde or dark, strong or weak. They pointed up personal oddities like red hair, funny feet, and crooked noses Oedipus means swollen-footed.

The early Greeks and Romans preferred single names. There were no first and last names.

This sometimes led to confusion. When one man became famous, other men "borrowed" his name. For instance, so many Greek poets called themselves Homer and wrote under that name that scholars aren't sure just which poems were written by **the** great Greek poet Homer.

The Romans had the naming system closest to our own. They combined a first name, a clan name, and a family name, as in Caius Julius Caesar.

Surnames fell with the Roman Empire. They didn't come back into common usage until around the time of the Norman Conquest, in the fifteenth century.

In 1465, King Edward of England ordered every man to take an English surname of "one town as Sutton, or color as Whyte, Black or Brown, or art of Science as Carpenter, or office as Cook or Butler," and to continue to hand the name down through his children.

By and large, these are the names still in use today. One may be your own.

INTERESTING NAME CUSTOMS

In Ghana, in Africa, the Ashantis name their children for the day of the week on which they were born. The naming is similar to the old nursery rhyme,

> "Monday's child is fair of face/
> Tuesday's child is full of grace/
> Wednesday's child is full of woe/
> Thursday's child has far to go/
> Friday's child is loving and giving/
> Saturday's child works hard for a living/
> But the child who's born on the Sabbath day/
> Is blithe and bonny and good and gay."

The not-so-odd thing is that Ashanti children tend to live up (or down) to their names. Monday's child, Swadwo, is expected to be quiet and good and usually is. Wednesday's child, Kwaku, is considered a born hell

DON'T TELL ME, I KNOW, YOUR FRIEND WAS BORN ON A WEDNESDAY.

raiser. As a consequence, there are more than twice as many Kwakus in trouble and in jail.

In Japan, children are sometimes given names that indicate birth order. Thus Ichiko is literally a number one child.

In China, parents used to give their children ugly, harsh sounding names. That way they wouldn't tempt the envy of the gods, who would then leave the children alone.

In Greece, the first boy is often named after the grandfather.

In Iceland, people are listed by their first name in the phone book.

In Sweden, different versions of the same family name are grouped in the phone book under the "official" spelling. Thus, if you wanted to find Carlson, you would look under Karlsson.

In Russia, children take their father's name as their middle name. They add either "ovich" (son of) or "ovna" (daughter of). Thus, Ivan names his son Igor, which makes him Igor Ivanovich, plus his last name.

MY NAME IS IVAN, AND YOURS IS IVANOVICH.

HOW COME MINE IS HARDER TO SPELL?

In **Spanish speaking countries,** husbands and wives both keep their mother's and father's names. (But only the father's name is passed on to the children.) If you meet a girl named Maria Lopez Martinez, the Lopez is from her father's name, while Martinez is her mother's name.

In **England,** a hyphenated last name is often used as a way of keeping the mother's name in the family, as in Anthony Armstrong-Jones.

In **America,** a hyphenated last name is most often a way of giving equal status to husband and wife, by honoring both names. Thus, Farrah Fawcett marries Lee Majors and becomes Farrah Fawcett-Majors.

MY NAME IS GERALDO LOPEZ MARTINEZ AFTER MY FATHER AND MY MOTHER.

IT'S NICE TO HONOR BOTH PARENTS.

Chapter Five
First Names

Where do first names come from? The Bible was, and is, a prime source.

Old Testament names like Sarah, Rachel, Hannah and Isaiah were favored by the Puritans. Mary is the most popular woman's name of all time. And the world is full of Matthews, Marks, Lukes and Johns.

The Hebrew ending "El" stands for God. Thus the popular boys names Michael, Daniel, Mañuel and Gabriel all have "God" in them, as do their feminine forms Michelle, Danielle, Mañuella and Gabrielle.

Some names come from mythology. Helen was the goddess of light. Dionysius (from which we get Dennis) was the god of revel and fun.

Some names come from tribes and places. The original Franks were a Germanic tribe who invaded Roman Gaul and turned it into present-day France. Lorraine is the name derived from a much fought over French-German border.

Other names come from animals. Leo and Lionel are lion names. Ursula is a wolf lady. Sitting Bull is a typical Indian name.

The early Germans and Hebrews both liked animal names. The Germans preferred the names of wild animals. For instance, Adolph means wolf and Rudolph is a red wolf, while Arnold is a strong eagle and Bertram a bright raven. The given name of the world famous composer, Wolfgang Mozart, literally means wolf-tread.

The Hebrews preferred to name after the tamer animals. Deborah is a bee, Rachel a ewe and Jonah a dove. Melissa, from the Greek, is also a bee.

Many of the Puritans named their children for virtues they hoped they would have. Patience, Prudence, Love, Charity and Chastity were common. These names are still used. Recently, popular singer Cher named her firstborn daughter Chastity.

Other Puritan parents laid on God-fearing names such as Sorry-for-Sin and Repentance, and the even heavier Through-Much-Tribulation-We-Enter-the-Kingdom-of Heaven. One Puritan father had three children named Return, Believe and Tremble.

Other early American names indicated special situations. The fourth or fifth girl born in a row might be named Hopestill, which meant the parents still hoped for a boy next. A child whose father died before birth might be called Fatherbegone.

A few first names come from mispronunciations of foreign names and phrases. Mabel comes from the French **ma bell,** which means my beautiful, while Amy comes from the French **aimée,** which means beloved.

John and Mary

Mary is the all-time favorite girl's name. It means wished-for child or star of the sea. Other forms are Molly, Polly, Miriam, Marion, Marie, Maureen, Maria, Mitzi, Mamie (as in Mamie Eisenhower) and Manon (as in the opera by that name).

John, the favorite boy's name, means God's gracious gift. The name has over 90 variants and appears in 27 different languages. A few are Evan (Welsh), Giovanni (Italian), Hans (Dutch), Ivan (Russian), Jan (Polish), Jens (Danish), Ian (Scottish), Sean (Irish), and Jean (French). Nicknames for John are Jack, Johnny and Jock.

There are also a number of non-human Johns. John Bull is a British symbol, John Doe is used in legal documents when the real name is unknown, a Johnny-come-lately is a person one step behind the times and a Johnny-on-the-spot is one who is right there in an emergency.

Putting your John Hancock on a letter means to sign it boldly and legibly. When John Hancock signed the Declaration of Independence, he made his signature so bold and big that King George of England could read it without glasses.

THE TOP TEN

The Most Popular First Names As
Recorded in New York City Birth Certificates

	Boys	Girls
1898	John	Mary
	William	Catherine
	Charles	Margaret
	George	Annie
	Joseph	Rose
	Edward	Marie
	James	Esther
	Louis	Sarah
	Francis	Frances
	Samuel	Ida
1948	Robert	Linda
	John	Mary
	James	Barbara
	Michael	Patricia
	William	Susan
	Richard	Kathleen
	Joseph	Carol
	Thomas	Nancy
	Stephen	Margaret
	David	Diane

1972	Michael	Jennifer
	David	Michelle
	Christopher	Lisa
	John	Elizabeth
	James	Christine
	Joseph	Maria
	Robert	Nicole
	Anthony	Kimberly
	Richard	Denise
	Brian	Amy
1977	Michael	Jennifer
	David	Jessica
	Joseph	Nicole
	John	Melissa
	Jason	Michelle
	Christopher	Elizabeth
	Anthony	Lisa
	Robert	Danielle
	James	Maria
	Daniel	Christine

NON-SEXIST NAMES

A number of names are spelled exactly the same way for boys and girls. Examples are Evelyn, Vivien, Marion, Leslie, Joyce, Florence, Jesse, Noel and Sidney. Others such as Frances (feminine) and Francis (masculine) and Emil (masculine) and Emily (feminine) have slight changes in spelling.

Is it a handicap for a boy to have a girlish sounding name?

Popular newspaper columnist Ann Landers thought so. She got a letter from a new father asking for advice. His wife, he said, wanted to name their baby Vivien after a much loved uncle and he was against the idea. What did she think? Would the boy's life be ruined if he was a Vivien?

Ann Landers' sensible suggestion was compromise. Name the child something like Michael Vivien and call him Mike. She added, "If you lose the battle, give Vivien a nickname early and teach him how to fight."

A surprising number of famous people have learned to do just that. John Wayne, the rough tough Western movie star, had Marion for a real first name. He was teased unmercifully. New teachers always put him wrongly in the girls' classroom. He hated it. But because of it, he learned to use his fists early and stick up for himself.

Winston Churchill was called Winnie. He, too, hated his girlish sounding name. As a child, it made him quiet and shy. As a grown-up, it gave him the confidence and strength that comes from overcoming and coping. During his long career, he felt better able to "take it" for having had to take it as a child.

In the popular song, "A Boy Named Sue," a father gives his son a girl's name on purpose. He figures a kid so named will **have** to learn to defend himself—or die. And he does grow stronger for it.

That's one tactic. Another is to laugh it off. This is almost impossible at first but gets easier with practice.

TWIN NAMES

Over 60% of twins have names that begin with the same initial: Jack and Jill, Ned and Nora, Roger and Rhoda, Ellen and Edna. Twin names also tend to balance in sound and number of syllables.

Sometimes only the beginning letter is changed, as in Delia and Celia, Flora and Dora, Donald and Ronald. Sometimes it is the last letter, as in Clark and Clara, Frances and Francis.

Parents give twins similar names because they are often alike. Even if they are not identical, they tend to be treated as a team.

The only bad effect on this is that later it may be more difficult for them to develop separate identities. Which is why other twin parents give names that are as opposite as possible, such as Madeline and Lisa, Stephen and Mark.

Then there are the funny twin names, like Max and Climax and their friends, Pete and Repeat. In England, a mother really did name her twin daughters Kate and Duplicate.

FIRST-NAME FADS

Some people think the more names the better, probably because long ago kings had many more names than commoners.

In 1880, an English girl named Pepper was given a name for every letter of the alphabet. Her full name was Anna Bertha Cecilia Diana Emily Fanny Gertrude Hypatia Inez Jane Kate Louise Maud Nora Ophelia Quince Rebecca Starkey Theresa Ulysis Venus Winifred Xenophone Yetty Zeno. She was called Annie.

Not to be topped, a Michigan mother with the last name of Kalofen named her daughter Aleatha Beverly Carol Diana Eva Felice Greta Harline Io Joanne Karen Laquite Maurine Naomi Orpha Patricia Queenie Rebecca Shirley Teresa Una Valeeta Wanda Xelia Yolanda Zoe. She asked everyone to call her Pat.

Some parents pick an initial letter and stick to it. Every member of the piano-playing Schrade family has a first name that begins with R: Robert and Rolande are the parents, Robelyn, Randolph, Rhonda, Rolisa and Rorianne their offspring. They call themselves the Sevenars.

Another neat trick is to name all the children so that their initials form their nickname. Which also makes for an interesting monogram. Thus, Kimberly Inez Morissey is K.I.M., Pamela Ann Morissey is P.A.M., and Thomas Otto Morissey is T.O.M.

Backwards-Forwards Names

A few first names are palindromes. That means the name is the same spelled backwards of forwards. It also means the name owner can boast about his instant ability to spell backwards.

Palindrome names are Otto, Anna, Hannah, Ada, Ava, Ede and Emme. Can you think of any others?

NEW TRENDS IN NAMING

One fairly recent trend that seems to be gaining in popularity is to use last names as first names. Many names such as Carter, Bertram, Herbert, Humphrey and Clark go both ways. Almost any pleasant sounding family name may be used as a given name. My son has three "last" names: his full name is Freeman Brackett Hazen.

Another trend is to combine two unusual first names into a new form. This may be a way of pleasing both grandparents or incorporating both parents' names.

Charlene is a name in itself. It may also be a purposeful combination of Charles and Lena, just as Joanna may be a combined form of Joe and Anna. Similarly, Marlyn is a fusion of Margaret and Carolyn; Adnell, of Addison and Nellie; and Romiette, of Romeo and Juliette.

There is an increase in the giving of nicknames as real names. Betty, Lisa, Vicky, Jack and Tom reflect a more casual age and appear on birth certificates today.

There is also an increase in unusual spellings of usual names—Viki instead of Vicky, Lynda instead of Linda, Neall insteal of Neal, and Maryruth, all run together.

Several trends have a particular significance. There is less differentiation between boys and girls names. Many of the currently most popular girls names—Danielle, Michelle and Nicole—are the feminine form of boys' names.

Ethnic names are increasingly popular. They reflect an increasing pride and interest in roots and origins. Today, more than ever, blacks are likely to give their children African names. A Latin family might choose Jose or Juanita; a child of Scandinavian heritage might be named Jens instead of the Americanized John.

Unique and made-up names are also increasingly popular. Some of these names are computer-born. Others come out of strong personal conviction. Conservation-concerned parents named their first born Tesa, combining the first letters of trees, earth, sun and air.

Some parents simply play with syllables and sounds until they happen upon a new name. Such a name is particularly personal. It is a way of saying this small person is special. There is no one in the world like him or her.

POPULAR GIRLS NAMES AND WHAT THEY SAY ABOUT YOU

Alice: Serene, sweet, somewhat shy.
Amy: Affectionate, old-fashioned tastes.
Ann, Anne and Annette: Fun, a friend you can count on.
Audrey: A born leader, could be a bit bossy.

Barbara: Spirited, curious, can be moody.
Bernice: Late bloomer, likes presents, quiet.
Beverly: Feminine, gets good grades.
Brenda: Strong-minded, athletic.

Candice (Candy): Pretty and full of sparkle, smart too.
Carmen: A live wire, full of jokes.
Carol: You can trust her, a real friend.
Caroline and Carolyn: Good sport, bubbly, always on the phone.
Catherine and Katherine : Graceful, has a relaxed and regal side.
Christine: Dainty, likes ballet and outdoor sports.

Danielle: Popular with boys and girls, pretty.
Dawn: Head in the clouds, romantic.
Deborah: Super all-around girl, confident.
Denise: A go-getter, leader.
Diana: Artistic, tendency to brag.
Dorothy: Ladylike, occasionally puts on airs.

Edith: A good helper, well-organized.
Eileen: Will try anything once, enthusiastic.
Elaine: Very popular, has people over to her place.
Elizabeth: Deep friendships, strong personality.
Ellen: Talks a lot, worth listening to.
Emily: Bright but timid.
Erica: Bright, tends to gossip.

Florence: Slow starter but good worker, creative.
Frances: Spirited, a natural leader.

Gayle and Gail: Likes parties, likes fun; good sense of humor.
Ginger: Cute, talkative.

Harriet: Quiet, good athlete, more good points than she realizes.
Helen: Charming, a self-starter.

Ida: You can count on her, smart too.
Irene: Well-coordinated, dainty.

Jacqueline: All-around girl, spirited.
Jane: Honest, sly sense of fun.
Janet: Class leader, writes well.
Jean: Bright, sometimes jealous.
Jennifer: Feminine, interesting.
Jessica: Artistic, full of zest.
Joyce: Eager to please, sometimes too eager.
Judith and Judy: Warm-hearted, giggly.
Julia and Juliet: Gutsy and sensitive.

Karen: Quick wit, quiet manner.
Kathleen: Full of fun, always invited.
Kim: Popular, sometimes headstrong.

Laura: Romantic, an edge of mystery.
Lilian: A light side and a secretive side, artistic.
Lisa: Top of her class, well-rounded and well-liked.
Lorraine: Gets others going, a good sport.
Lucy: Bright, often acts more scatterbrained than she is.

Madeline: Graceful, studious.
Marcia: Talks a lot, loves to eat.
Margaret and Margot: Sweet, but has a quick temper.
Mary: A very together person, popular.
Martha: You can count on her friendship and work.
Melissa: Always buzzing about, high-spirited.
Michelle: Dynamic, a good dancer.

Nancy: A lot goes on under the surface, thoughtful.
Nicole: Shy, with a special sparkle.

Olga: Good organizer, reads a lot.

Patricia: Likes sports and games, a leader.
Paula: Feminine, stubborn side.
Penny: Pretty, doesn't always stick to things.

Rachel: Quiet, but has a special warmth.
Rebecca: Popular, a flair for the dramatic.
Rhoda: Good organizer, sharp wit.
Ruth: Enjoys her friends, has lots of energy.

Sally: Zany sense of humor, very popular.
Sandra: Bright, may take herself too seriously.
Sara and Sarah: Lovely, sensitive to others.
Sophia and Sophie: Full of vim and vigor, pretty.
Stacey: Good-looking, has a tendency to brag.
Stephanie: Good all-round personality, fast starter.
Susan: Lively, exceptionally well liked.

Tammy: High-spirited, sometimes gets into trouble.
Theresa: Feminine, has a stubborn streak.
Tracey: Active, energetic, likes to have friends over.

Ursula: Strong-minded, likes to take charge.

Valerie: A people person, always in the center of
things.
Victoria and Vicky: Many sided, fanciful and bright
too.
Vivian: Gets things done, may be moody.

" IF YOU'RE
A GIRL WHOSE
NAME IS NOT
INCLUDED IN
THIS LIST—YOU
ARE NO DOUBT
ROMANTIC
AS WELL AS
PRACTICAL! "

POPULAR BOYS NAMES AND WHAT THEY SAY ABOUT YOU

Adam: Good sport, hard worker.
Allen: Thoughtful, well-liked.
Andre: Wise beyond his years, good looking.
Andrew (Andy): One of the boys, very popular.
Anthony: A go-getter, natural leader.
Arnold: Quiet, studious, good personality.
Arthur: Kids around a lot, class clown.

Barry: Likes to be first, personable.
Benjamin: Quiet side predominates, has a sense of humor.
Bill: Hard worker, all-around boy.
Brian: Bright, leads the gang in pranks.
Bruce: Nature lover, independent.

Charles: Large circle of friends, somewhat easygoing.
Chester: Strong, tendency to bully.
Christopher: Sophisticated and smart.

Daniel: Sensitive, but sometimes doesn't do his share.
David: Very special, very well liked, trustworthy.
Derrick: Likes parties and sports, witty.
Donald: Smooth talker, hard worker, has a temper.
Douglas: Energetic, gets things done.

Edgar: Serious, bright, can't always take a joke.
Edward: Considerate, fun to be with.
Ernest: Practical, good at making things.
Eugene: Well liked, sometimes goofs off.

Francis: Independent, a nature lover.
Frank: Forceful, sticks up for what he wants.
Fred: Clever, likes cars.

Gary: Popular, kids around a lot.
George: Always on the move, a class leader.
Gregory: Handsome, everybody wants to be his friend.

Harold: Cautious, does things his own way.
Herbert: Likes outdoor sports, strong willed.
Henry and Harry: High-spirited, will try anything once.

James: Smart and popular, head of the class.
Jason: Has a large circle of friends, artistic.
Jeffrey: A go-getter and prankster.
Jerry: Easygoing, good sense of fun.
John: Great personality, sometimes lazy.

Keith: Ambitious, good at math.
Kenneth: Energetic, good joke teller.
Kirk: A real ringleader, everybody's friend.

Lance: Skinny, athletic, not very talkative.
Lawrence (Larry): Manly, sometimes moody.
Louis: Aristocratic, likes to spend money.

Mark: A live wire, sometimes brags.
Matthew: Thoughtful friend, hard worker.
Michael: Likes animals and causes, very masculine.

Neal: Born winner, top of the class.
Nelson: Good organizer, lots of friends.
Nicholas: Strong willed, well liked.

Oliver: Very bright, tends to act as if he knows it.

Patrick: Thoughtful, has lots of good ideas.
Paul: Trustworthy, good company.
Peter: Ambitious, successful, full of zest.
Philip: Good looking, very popular.

Randolph (Randy): A leader, sometimes pushes others around.
Richard: Attractive, acts as if he knows it.
Robert: A good friend, tendency to be shy.
Ronald: Smart, but sometimes slides by.
Russell: Manly, girls go for him.

Samuel (Sam): Slow starter but deep thinker.
Scott: A winner, gets top marks.
Sheldon (Shelley): Cautious, logical mind.
Stephen and Steven: All-around-good-guy, popular.
Stewart and Stuart: Good at sports, independent.

Theodore: Exceptionally clever, likes music.
Thomas: Teases a lot, popular, sometimes puts things off.
Tyler: Full of zest, likes to go places.

Victor: Confident, well-coordinated, likes contact sports.

Ward: Full of clever ideas, fun to be with.
Walter: Bright, may take himself too seriously.
William: Good instincts, makes a good friend.

Zachary: Tough guy outside, sensitive inside.

" IF YOU'RE A BOY WHOSE NAME IS NOT INCLUDED IN THIS LIST— YOU ARE NO DOUBT ATHLETIC AS WELL AS STUDIOUS!"

Chapter Six
Middle Names

Middle names are the neglected members of the name family. They are often dropped. They are seldom said. They are a way of naming you after Aunt Hermione or Uncle Herman without your ever having to be called that.

They are also a way of bringing in the mother's side of the family. A maiden name that is pleasing becomes a middle name, as in Lyndon **Baines** Johnson and Barbara **Foster** Shook.

Too many middle names are like excess baggage. Too weird a middle name can be an embarrassment. Often they are the names you don't tell except to your very best friend.

Historically, middle names haven't been in use long. Only three of the original signers of the Declaration of Independence had middle names: Francis

Lightfoot Lee, Richard Henry Lee and Robert Treat Paine. Of the first 17 presidents, only John Quincy Adams had a middle name. The name Quincy was for his father's best friend.

Some people never use their middle names. Some never admit to them. A number of people use just the initial, as in George M. Cohan.

Many women drop their middle names after marriage. They use their maiden name instead as a middle name, as in Barbara Shook Hazen instead of Barbara Jean Shook Hazen.

Is there any advantage to having a middle name, other than pleasing Grandma while calling you something else?

Often they add a touch of class. Edgar Allen Poe has a far more impressive ring than just Edgar Poe. Middle names also add an uncommon note to common names. John Russell Smith sounds and looks more distinctive than John Smith.

Perhaps most important, middle names give their owners a choice. If you can't stand your first name, switch to your middle name.

If you don't want to be called by your first name but still want to keep it in mind, you can use your first-name initial plus the middle name. An impressive number of important people have done just that. F. Scott Fitzgerald, J. Pierpont Morgan and J. Edgar Hoover are good examples. Such names sound special. And, more often than not, their owners are.

Another possibility is to use your first and middle name as one long name. This is particularly true in the South. Thus you are known by both names, as Barbara Jean, Lonni Sue, Emmy Lou or John Allen.

This is not the same as the little girl who only thought she had a double name because every time her mother called her, she called, "Mary, MARY!"

Occasionally an initial is a middle name. President Harry S. Truman had two sets of grandparents. One was named Shippe, the other Solomon. His clever parents used an S to cover both bases. Both families could believe the S stood for them. Actually it stood for nothing, which led to many jokes years later when political opponents called him Harry S Stands For Nothing.

Finally, a middle name increases the likelihood that your initials will spell a word. In England, this is thought lucky. And it is, if your name is Joyce Olga Yeats. J.O.Y. looks great on a sweater or suitcase. It is not so great if your name happens to be Ann Sara Smilgen, Peter Ivan Gregory or Samuel Owen Brewster.

Chapter Seven
Last Names

Until the last five hundred years or so, people were known by their first names. They had no last names. They didn't need them because there weren't that many people in the world.

As population increased, so did the confusion. First names weren't enough to differentiate between one person and another. There also weren't enough different ones.

The first last names were strictly personal names that died with their owner. They were not passed down, father to son.

A few noblemen also had last names. These were called "Sir" names. From them we get the word surname, which today means last name.

Last names came into common use after the Norman Conquest. They identified and differentiated between John the smithy (who became John Smith) and John the garment maker (who became John Taylor). When there were two Roberts in the town, they made it instantly apparent which one you were talking about or taking a letter to—Robert Long or Robert Short. They avoided any confusion between the Mary who lived on high land (Mary Hill) and Mary who lived in the valley (Mary Dale).

They are fascinating clues as to what a person's ancestors looked like, what they did and where they came from.

DESCRIPTIVE NAMES

The earliest last names came from obvious personal characteristics. Swarthy Edward became known as Black Edward, which differentiated him from his fair-haired cousin. As family names came increasingly into use, a number of these were simply switched around. Swarthy Edward became Edward Black; his cousin Edward White, or Lilywhite, or Whitelock, or even Fairchild. There is also Brown, Grey, and Reed or Reid, both of which mean red.

Long, Short, Slight and Small refer to body build. So do Littlehead and Longshanks. In France, Monsieur Legrand is literally Mr. Big.

"I LIKE WHAT THE FRENCH CALL ME."

MONSIEUR LEGRAND

Names such as Goode, Moody, Smart and Reckless reflected personality traits. Drinkwater, All-work and Whistler reflect their owners' habits.

Animals provided another name source. A man who thought himself clever might become a Fox. A strong he-man might take the name Bear (or Baer, Bahr, Barnard or Barret). There are Cranes and Crows, Lions and Lambs, Lambs and Wolfs, and Wolfsons, the sons of Wolfs. Less obvious, any Adler is an eagle, Fogelman means bird man, and Columbus was a dove man.

Match the Last Names With
What They Say About the Person.

Bonaparte	has a crooked nose
Schwartz	big-headed
Fairfax	trustworthy hard worker
Curtis	lazy
Doolittle	red-haired
Kennedy	polite
Klein	dark
Calvin	bald
Cameron	right-handed
Rodriguez	little
Truman	fair-skinned

Bonaparte is right-handed, Schwartz is dark, Fairfax is light-skinned, Curtis is polite, Doolittle is lazy, Kennedy is big-headed, Klein is little, Calvin is bald, Cameron has a crooked nose, Rodriguez is red-headed and Truman is a trusted hard worker.

OCCUPATIONAL NAMES

Many people took names that reflected what they did. There were, and still are, numerous Bakers, Butlers, Barbers, Brewers, Carpenters, Caterers, Cooks, Clarks and Farmers.

There were Masons but no Bricklayers, because stone, not brick, was used at the time. Similarly, there were Butchers but no Grocers, and Bellmen but no Mediamen.

Some occupational names are not the exact words we use today. Eisenhower was an iron worker and LaGuardia a guard. Webster (the weaver) wove the material which Taylor (the tailor) made into a suit which Chapman (the merchant) then sold to Badger (who transported it by barge). In the building trade, Foster or Forester went out into the woods to fetch the wood which Boardman cut into boards so that Wainwright could build his wagon. The church and nobility were represented by Abbot, Cardinal, Duke, Earl, Prince and King.

More recent occupational names reflect the changing times. Fifty years ago when the Shah of Iran decreed that everyone in the country take a last name, people became Plumbers and Engineers as well as Bakers and Kings.

The most popular name in the world was, and still is, Smith. There is a good reason. The name itself means metal worker or smithy. When last names were being taken, metalworkers made the weapons that protected the towns and villages. The smithy was an important, respected person. Thus each community acquired a Smith.

Today there are millions of Smiths in the world. It is, by far, the most common English name. In French, it becomes Lefevre or Faure; in German, Feuer or Schmidt; in Russian, Kuznetsov; and in Spanish, Ferraro.

There are also Goldsmiths, Silversmiths and Arrowsmiths.

Sometimes, because the name is so common, Smiths acquire very unusual first names. In the social security rolls there is a 1½ Smith, an Oddball Smith as well as an Aaaaaaaay Smith.

There is even a Smith joke: John Smith saw a bank robbery and offered to be a witness. When the police arrived on the scene, the officer asked the witness his name.

"John Smith," said the man.

"I want your **real** name," said the policeman.

"John Smith," the man repeated.

"Cut the comedy," snarled the policeman. "I asked for and want your REAL name."

"Okay," the weary man sighed. "Just put me down as Jimmy Carter."

"Now that's more like it," said the beaming policeman. "You can't kid me with that John Smith stuff."

FATHER (OR PATRONYMIC) NAMES

In biblical times, Isaac was known as the son of Abraham. More recently, Davidson is the son of David and Robertson is Robert's son. This is quite obvious.

But Davis and Davison are also David's sons. And Robinson, Hobbs and Dobbs are sons of Robert. The connection in the last instance is that they rhyme with Rob, a diminutive form of Robert.

In the same manner, from Richard and its diminutive Dick come all the following: Richardson, Dickerson, Dickens, Dix, Hicks, Dixon (Dick's son) and Nixon. Thus, ex-President Richard Nixon might well have been called Dick Dick.

Somewhat harder to figure out are Watson (Walter's son), Tennyson (Dennis's son), Benson (Benjamin's son), Sanderson (Alexander's son), and Harrison (the son of a Henry whose nickname is Harry).

"IF DAVID IS THE FATHER OF DAVIDSON—WHO IS ROBERTSON'S FATHER?"

MOTHER (OR MATRONYMIC) NAMES

Not all last names come from the father's side of the family. Babson is the son of a Barbara, Nelson the son of a Nell and Nanson is clearly Nan's son.

In Spanish, Jimenéz is a last name derived from the feminine Jimena. In Italy, artist Paolo della Francesca's name proudly pronounced that he was Paul the son of Frances.

"IF NAN IS THE MOTHER OF NANSON — WHO IS NELSON'S MOTHER?"

FIND OUT ABOUT YOUR FRIENDS.

Do any of them have names similar to those below?

Ander**sen** = Ander's son (Scandinavian)
Martin**ez** = Martin's son (Spanish)
de Stefano = Steven's son (Italian)
Ivan**of** = Ivan's son (Russian)
O'Henry = Henry's son (Irish-of)
MacDonald = Donald's son (Scottish)
ben Gurion = Gurion's son (Hebrew)
Adam**s** = Adam's son (English-
           possessive case)
Jones = John's son (Welsh pronunciation)

PLACE NAMES

A John who lived high on a hill might acquire the name John Hill, or Hillman, or Hilton, if he lived in a hilly town.

Similarly, Atwell lived near the town well. Atwood, Bywood and Woods lived somewhere out in the woods.

Brooks, Riviera, Atwater, and Bathurst all lived near the water. So did Gerald Ford's ancestors.

The original Roosevelts must have resided near a rose filled field, while Winston Churchill's ancestors likely lived on a hill whose peak had a church. Greenberg boasts of living in a town with a good rainfall, and Bradley once must have lived on a broad lea (word for meadow).

Other place names identify their owners as coming from a certain village, city or country. The most important family in any village was likely to take the name of the village. The name spread when some of the sons moved on, taking the name with them and continuing it through their sons.

The orgins of writers Jack London and Anatole France and Judge Felix Frankfurter are clear. That Walt Disney's family came from Isigny, a small town in France, is not so obvious. Do you or any of your friends have place names?

WHAT YOUR LAST NAME BEGINS WITH AND DOES IT AFFECT YOUR LIFE

If your last name is Adams are you likely to do better in school than a Young or Zuckerman?

Trevor Weston, a British doctor, thinks so. In a study, he found that people whose names began with **S-Z** were less likely to succeed and more likely to get sick. He called the problem Alphabetical Neurosis. He claimed it came from always waiting for your name to be called, from always being last in line.

He named those born with names starting beyond **R**, the S-Z Club. He suggested that members suffered from constant anxiety in the classroom. During an oral quiz, for instance, the **A's** and **B's** not only got first crack at the answer but might take your answer. They also were seated first at lunch and might help themselves to your food.

Another survey, my own informal one, came to the conclusion that it doesn't much matter. As one young man put it, "Sometimes it's a little annoying. But most of the time, it gives me longer to think up an answer."

Which is the beginning letter of the largest number of last names? **S**, by far, followed by **B, M, K,** and **D. X** marks last place.

THE FIRST FIFTY

The Most Common Surnames According to a Recent Social Security Survey. Note the large number of patronymics.

1	Smith	2,382,509
2	Johnson	1,807,263
3	Williams & Williamson	1,568,939
4	Brown	1,362,910
5	Jones	1,331,205
6	Miller	1,131,205
7	Davis	1,047,848
8	Martinez & Martinson	1,046,297
9	Anderson	825,648
10	Wilson	787,825
11	Harrison	754,083
12	Taylor	696,046
13	Moore	693,304
14	Thomas	688,054
15	White	636,185
16	Thompson	635,426
17	Jackson	630,003
18	Clark	549,107
19	Roberts & Robertson	524,688
20	Lewis	495,026
21	Walker	486,498
22	Robinson	484,991

23	Peterson	479,249
24	Hall	471,479
25	Allen	458,375
26	Young	455,416
27	Morris & Morrison	455,179
28	King	434,791
29	Wrightson	431,157
30	Nelson	421,638
31	Rodriguez	416,178
32	Hill	414,646
33	Baker	412,676
34	Richards & Richardson	409,262
35	Lee	409,068
36	Scott	408,439
37	Green	406,989
38	Adams	406,841
39	Mitchell	371,434
40	Phillips	362,013
41	Campbell	361,958
42	Gonzales & Gondalez	360,994
43	Carter	349,950
44	Garcia	346,175
45	Evans	343,897
46	Turner	329,752
47	Stewart	329,581
48	Collins	324,680
49	Parker	317,197
50	Edward	312,186

The Long and Short Of It

The Longest Name:
Adolph Blaine Charles David Earl Frederick Gerald
Hubert Irvin John Kenneth Lloyd Martin Nero Oliver
Paul Quincy Randolph Sherman Thomas Uncas
Victor William Xerxes Yancy Zeus Wolfeschlegelstein-
hausenbergerdorffvoralternawarengewissen-
haftschaferswessenschafewar-
enwohlgepflegeundsorgfaltigkeitbeschutzenvon-
angreifendurchihrraubgierigfeingdewelchevor-
alternzwolftausendjarhresvoran-
dierscheinenvanderersteerdemenschderraum-
schiffgebrauchlichtalkreisedrehensichundwohindern-
eurassevonverstandigmenschlich-
keitkonntefortpflanzenundsicherfreuenan-
lebenslanglichfreudeundruhemitnich-
teinfurchtvorangreifenvonanderintelligentgeschopf-
svonhinzwischensternartigraum, Senior.

He called himself Hubert Wolf + 590, Senior.

The Shortest:
U Nu from the United Nations.
Lok Yu who lives in New York City.
Monsieur O a native of France.

Chapter Eight
Nicknames

The word nickname comes from the root "eke," which means additional. A nickname is an extra name in addition to your real name.

What it is **not** is what is on your birth certificate. If the name registered on your birth certificate is Lisa or Jack, then it is your real name not your nickname, even though Lisa is often a nickname for Elizabeth and the majority of Jacks are really Johns.

Nicknames have been around for a long time. A Roman consul born before Christ was nicknamed "Stupid" by discontented cronies. The ancient Roman poet Ovid was nicknamed "Flaccus," for flabby. Sophocles was nicknamed "the Bee"; Homer, "the Prince of Poets."

Nicknames can be affectionate, gently teasing or downright belittling. A large number are descriptive. Such nicknames range from Red to Stubby and Shorty to Ape-face. Some stick with their owners for a lifetime, but others, like Ape-face, we hope do not.

Many nicknames are informal or short (diminutive) forms of first names—Bob, Bobby or Rob for Robert; Chuck or Charlie for Charles; Beth, Betty or Liz for Elizabeth.

Margaret may have the largest number of nicknames. There's Madge, Maisie, Maggie, Meg, Peggy, Peg and Daisy, because in French Marguerite means daisy. There are also Rita, Gretchen (German), Margot, Marjorie, and Marguerita (Spanish), which are also used as given names.

Some nicknames come from last names. A MacDonald, McDorman or MacGruder often ends up "Mac" or "Mack." A Smith becomes Smitty; a Jones, Jonesey; a Willoughby, Will.

The great British statesman Disraeli was nicknamed Dizzy. Poet John Keats was telescoped into "Junkets." Comedian Bob Hope was called Hopeless as a child.

A surprising number of nicknames stick throughout their owner's lifetimes. Harry Lillis Crosby was called Bing after his favorite comic strip, **Bingville Bugle.**

Pianist Edward Ellington got the nickname Duke because, as a young man, his clothes were elegant, his manners charming. Today he is known as Duke Ellington.

Another lifelong Duke was actor John Wayne. He got his nickname not because of his manner but because of his dog, Duke. Together they were known as Big Duke (the dog) and Little Duke (John Wayne as a little boy).

In his elementary school days FBI man J. Edgar Hoover earned the nickname Speed. He worked as a delivery boy after school and was such a fast runner that he earned over $2.00 a day, big money in those days. He carried the bags an average of two miles for each 10¢ tip!

Circumstance shapes some nicknames. Presidents Filmore and Tyler were both nicknamed "His Accidency" because they became president due to a predecessor's death. "Toni Ducks" was the nickname of criminal Antonio Corallo. He was good at ducking convictions since he was arrested 13 times but only convicted twice.

MY NICKNAME IS 'BYE-BYE' BECAUSE I ALWAYS HAVE MY TRUNK WITH ME.

Occasionally a nickname is acquired because of a child's inability to correctly pronounce the real name. Queen Elizabeth of England acquired her nickname Lilibet because her little sister couldn't cope with the **e**'s and **z.**

Nicknames are good confusion avoiders when several members of the family have the same name, particularly when there is a junior. If the father is called Charles, the son becomes Charlie or Chuck. One family, with a tradition of naming all firstborn girls Theodosia, alternated the nicknames Theo and Dosia. If the grandmother was called Theo, her daughter would be called Dosia, while **her** daughter would be Theo again.

PET NAMES

Pet names are even more familiar than nicknames. They are the affectionate names used only within the family and between best friends.

But mostly they are used in boy-girl relationships. Thus a boy may call his girl Kitten (but not Cat), Mouse (but not Rat) and Doll (but not Dummy).

WHO IS MOST LIKELY TO BE NICKNAMED?

Someone whose real name is long or difficult. Which is why my Aunt Union Forever was called Una and a Maximillian will likely end up Max.

School chums and best friends. A nickname is a sign of closeness. It shows you know the person, which is why you don't nickname strangers. A psychological study also showed that someone who acquires a nickname is better liked and better adjusted than someone who doesn't. A nickname is personal. It singles you out. Even if you don't relish the name, it shows people know you are around. Sports personalities tend to be known by nicknames. Pete Rose is "Charlie Hustle," and Babe Ruth was "The Sultan of Swat," while Joe DiMaggio was "The Yankee Clipper." The sports world is relaxed and easy, and so are most of the names used in it.

Often the name is set to its owner's image. Basketball star Walt Frazier began calling himself Clyde after the badman in the movie "Bonnie and Clyde," and after he, too, started wearing gangster-type clothes. Said he, "My nickname fits my style on the court: stealing and gambling and dribbling behind my back to escape pursuers."

Many politicians have nicknames like Irv and Ray and Sam. President Carter prefers the informal Jimmy to James. He, like a number of other people in public office, feels that casual is closer to the public. Some nicknames are downright folksy, like the Governor of Texas known as Pass the Biscuits Pappy O'Daniel.

Country singers and TV personalities lean toward nicknames for much the same reason. Country singing stars go by country casual nicknames like Willie, Johnny, Dolly and Jessie. Top TV talk show-hosts are Johnny and Merv and Dave. It is ironic that Barbara Walters, who always wanted to be called Babs, never was. What the relaxed nicknames suggest is an easy intimacy with the audience.

The underworld is also full of nicknames. "Scarface" Al Capone, Billy the Kid, and Murry "the Gimp" Wildcat Williams are among the more colorful criminal names.

WHAT TO DO IF YOU DON'T LIKE YOUR NICKNAME

Psychologists suggest: ignore it or try to laugh it off. Don't make an even bigger deal by blowing up every time you are called the nickname.

If it's a form of your real name, you can help by **telling** teachers and friends what you want to be called, Terrence not Terry, Betty not Betts. Start calling yourself that and signing your papers that way. Some people learn to live with their nicknames, as Lady Bird Johnson did. Even though for a long time she preferred Claudia.

Nasty nicknames hurt for a while, but at least they show people are aware of you. A cool approach is best, coupled with humor.

Happily such names have a way of changing as their owners change. There are few Froggies or Fatsos in the adult world.

THEY CALL ME FATSO— BUT I KNOW THEY LOVE ME.

FAMOUS EARLY AMERICANS AND THEIR NICKNAMES

Andrew Jackson = Old Hickory
James K. Polk = Young Hickory
Benjamin Harrison = Little Ben
William Henry Harrison = Old Tippecanoe
Charles Fremont = The Pathfinder
Thomas Jefferson = The Sage of Monticello
Henry Lee = Light-Horse Harry
Abraham Lincoln = The Rail Splitter,
                 also Martyr President
General Zachary Taylor = Old Rough and Ready
Noah Webster = The Schoolmaster of the Republic

Chapter Nine
Name Changing

At one time or another more than half the people in the world have wanted to change their name—first, last or both. Sometimes the feeling is deep-seated; other times it is fleeting and/or depends on circumstances.

Your name is one of the things about you that **can** be changed. Often it makes a big difference.

Tommy Wilson was a frail insecure mama's boy. He wasn't liked by the girls. He wasn't one of the boys. By the time he got to college, he was so unhappy and unhealthy that he dropped out.

That was when young Tommy Wilson decided it was time for a change—of image and name. He grew sideburns and sported snappier clothes. He began to use his middle name, which happened to be Woodrow. As Woodrow Wilson, he regained his health and grew in self-confidence and ambition. Later, he became president of the country.

Another young man who hated his name was Stephen B. Cleveland. When he was in his teens, he switched to Grover. He, too, became president.

There is nothing wrong with changing your name. It can be far better for your mental health than being constantly called something you can't stand.

Even the great Sigmund Freud, father of psychiatry, changed his first name—from Sigismund to Sigmund.

Well-known nutritionist Carlton Fredericks was born Harold Casper Frederick Caplan. He hated his name so much that, at age 9, he insisted his mother have it legally changed. He picked Carlton, a well-liked cousin's name, because it had an important ring. Carlton's name-change changed his self-esteem from low to high. And, as he felt more important, he became more important.

Many people don't exactly hate their name, but don't like it much either. Others hate their name when they are young and grow increasingly fond of it. A name that starts out as a source of kidding may end up a source of pride.

100

Moreover, there can be positive benefits from having negative feelings about your name. Author Alvin Toffler feels that having a name he was unhappy with made him better able to take stress. Both Dwight Eisenhower and Winston Churchill felt they grew into stronger men for having had to cope with childhood kidding. Bob Hope credits being called "Hopeless" with helping to hone his sense of humor.

Almost all people go through periods of wanting to be called something else. A girl named Nancy gets her close friends to call her Heidi for a while—just to see how it feels to be someone else. A boy named Charles asks to be called Chuck now that he's going out for the team. Casual Chuck sounds more like a football player.

A number of others alter the spelling of their real name. Mary becomes Mari while Mary Ruth fuses both names into Maryruth.

Moving and going to a new school are times when names are most likely to be tampered with. A new name gives the feeling of a fresh start.

" YOUR HONOR—BECAUSE I HAVE A REMARKABLE MEMORY, I WANT TO CHANGE MY NAME TO BOB HOPE SO THAT I CAN SING "THANKS FOR THE MEMORY."

UNITED HARVEYS AND MELVINS

Some names, more than others, become the butt of jokes. Harvey has been the name of an invisible rabbit in a play, another name for a "square," and the name of a bumbling cartoon character.

The last straw for one Harvey, a New York public relations executive, was when he realized there were three TV commercials (soup, soap and mouthwash) running simultaneously which portrayed Harveys as fumbling dolts.

He decided to do something about it and whipped off letters to 150 prominent fellow Harveys, including Harvey Firestone, a tire manufacturer, and pianist Van Cliburn, a closet Harvey (Harvey Lavan Cliburn) to see if they felt the same way.

They did. So much so that he got 127 supportive letters and $230 in unsolicited contributions.

This was the beginning of the pro-Harvey movement, which ended up with over four thousand members. The resulting Harvey power caused all three offending commercials to be dropped. The group also established a Fathers of a Harvey Award for the truest portrayal of a fictional character named Harvey. The winner: a movie character called Harvey Middleman Fireman, who "spryly depicted in human and humorous terms the vigorous yet fallible, but always manly characteristics of a Harvey."

A comedian brought about the Melvin crisis. Jerry Lewis once impersonated a fool whom he called Melvin. This caused the birth rate of Melvins to drop drastically. No parent wanted to give his child such a foolish-sounding name.

From the already existing Melvins there was a flood of protesting letters—such a flood that Jerry Lewis ended up apologizing publicly to all the Melvins of the world. Ironically, he considered changing the character's name to Harvey. He reconsidered and dropped the whole idea.

THE MAIN REASONS
FOR NAME CHANGING

It's long, difficult to spell or impossible to pronounce. Which means that nobody ever gets it right.

Someone you can't stand has the same name. Or someone overly famous. Like the little boy named George Washington who applied for an after-school job and was told, "My you certainly have a well-known name."

"I should have," he replied. "I've lived here all my life."

Because of unfortunate associations. A buck-toothed boy named Alvin is a candidate for kidding. Vaseline and Placenta (real first names) sound lovely but bring up unlovely mental pictures.

Because of something you strongly believe in. Which is why California feminist Ellen Cooperman became Cooperperson.

The most important reason: Because it doesn't feel like or fit you. Because you deeply dislike it every time you are called it or see it written down. And because it is a real impediment to your personal growth.

FUNNY NAMES UNFUNNY TO THEIR OWNERS

A man named Frankenstein changed his last name because he was sick and tired of people calling and asking to speak to the monster.

A man named Damn changed his when someone printed a picture of the whole Damn family.

A psychiatrist named Looney asked to have his name changed to Lowney. A Rotten man sought to legally become a Wroghton.

A thrifty Dutch immigrant named Van der Veer had his name legally changed to Vandever to save two words in cable charges.

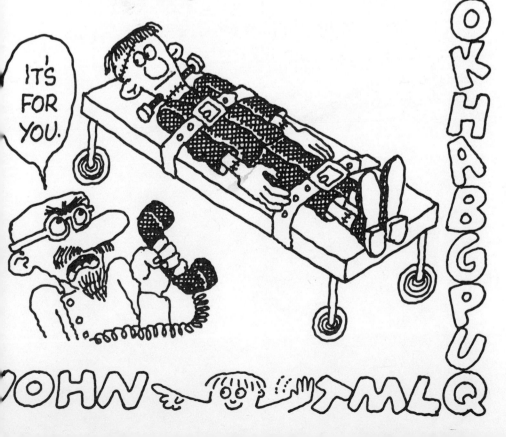

IT'S FOR YOU.

Chapter Ten
Your Name and the Law

Every state has different laws regarding a legal change of name. Generally it is not a very complicated legal process.

It is rare for the request for a name change to be turned down. But it does happen—as when a certain Earl Bottomlee wished to legally switch to Aerlygodlet Wileyelectronspirit Leegravity. The judge refused, ruling that the proposed change would be more a handicap than an improvement.

In some states, the name you are known by becomes your common law name. If your real registered name is Bettina Swivelwitch but you call yourself Betty Smith (and your friends call you that too), a will signed as Betty Smith will be legal.

Many people change their names slightly or informally. One starts using his middle name instead of his first name. Another alters Caroline to Carolyn.

But unless legally changed, Caroline will still be on the passport and social security papers. This could result in computer and person confusion. This is why it is a good idea, if you change your name drastically, to change it legally.

WOMEN NAMES

Today, an increasing number of women keep their maiden name after marriage, for both personal and professional reasons. Many also take it back legally after getting a divorce.

A number of women incorporate their maiden name with their married name to make a hyphenated double name. Mary Randall marries Howard Jones and becomes Mary (Mrs. Howard) Randall-Jones.

Hawaii is the only state in the union where the marriage license has separate spaces for the surnames of both husband and wife. There, about 10% of women being married either keep their name or hyphenate their name with their new husband's.

The first woman to insist on keeping her own name was a suffragette named Lucy Stone. She set the standard, and any woman who follows her footsteps is known as a Lucy Stoner.

IN OTHER COUNTRIES

In England the government has ruled that birth registrars have no legal right to interfere with the names parents pick for their children unless the name is "distinctly objectionable." "Not Wanted" was the name that brought on the first ruling.

Poland has a law allowing anyone with a ludicrous or humiliating name to get a new one and a fresh start. A person named Kielbasa (which is a kind of sausage) might well wish to switch.

In Sweden in the sixties, anyone with an overused name, such as Anderson, Karlsson, Johansson or Petersson, had the option of getting a unique brand-new computer-made-up name beginning witn the same initial. Syllables were fed the computer. It spit forth over 900,000 new names! This was immensely helpful because one firm alone in Sweden had 120 Andersons.

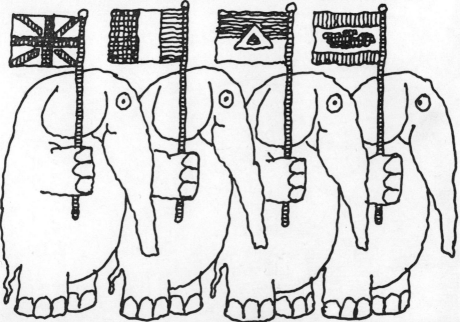

Name Changing Humor

And Did You Hear the One About:

The struggling actor who changed his last name to Exit so he could see his name in lights.

The ardent traveler who changed hers to Hilton so she could have personalized towels.

The man named Bridges who changed his first name to Narrow so he could brag that most of the bridges he crossed were named after him.

Chapter Eleven
Star Names

How do the superstars get their names? Errol Flynn, Mary Martin, John Travolta, Eartha Kitt and Zazu Pitts are all musical, memorable names, short enough to fit on a theatre marquee. They are also all real names.

Increasingly actors are opting to keep their real names, warts and all. Actress Cloris Leachman refused to change hers even though it was suggested it sounded like a laundry detergent. Humphrey Bogart kept his even though it brought him a lot of bad teasing as a child. It didn't help that he was forced to wear long, golden curls.

A number of stars keep threads and snatches of their real names but jazz them up. Richard Starkey becomes Ringo Starr of Beatle fame. Theodosia Goodman becomes Theda Bara the vamp.

Some take their middle names or borrow the names of relatives, which helps preserve some sense of former identity. Gladys Marie Smith became Mary Pickford, a slightly different form of her middle name, plus a cousin's last name.

Many and meandering are the routes to a star's name. Tuesday Weld born on a Thursday and christened a Susan. But her mother thought she looked more like a Tuesday and started calling her that. Later she legally changed her name to Tuesday.

Doris Day and Dinah Shore both got their names from songs they particularly liked to sing, "Day by Day," and "Dinah." Folk singer Phoebe Snow got hers from the name on the side of an Erie Lackawanna freight train car that used to pass by her New Jersey home. Englebert Humperdinck borrowed his from a 19th century German composer he admired. James Woodward became songster Tom Jones, capitalizing on the current popularity of a movie by the same name.

Elton John's real name was Reginald Dwight. Just before his first big hit record came out, he said, "It can't have Reg Dwight plastered all over it. Reg Dwight sounds like a cement mixer." So he took Elton from a sax player named Elton Dean and John from a buddy. Later he said that the change of name initiated a change of personality. It helped him get over the terrible sense of inferiority he had had since childhood.

114

Hometown pride is another name source. Famous opera singer Nellie Melba's name was inspired by her birthplace, Melbourne, Australia.

A much admired person is still another source. Enrich Weiss, 17, a poor Hungarian immigrant's son, Americanized his first name to Henry and took his last name from Robert Houdin, a magician, who was his hero. As Henry Houdini, he became the most famous trickster of all time.

The theatre wasn't always held in high regard. Herbert Blythe changed his name to Maurice Barrymore so as not to embarrass his family. They did not consider acting a "real" profession, but he far preferred the glitter of the footlights to the glare of his lawbooks. He became head of the greatest acting family ever, the Barrymore clan.

Many star names are made up by studio heads. Tab Hunter and Rock Hudson are typical manufactured names. Marion Michael Morrison was renamed John Wayne by a producer, who found Marion too girlish, Michael too Irish and Morrison too long. John Wayne had just the right all-American he-man ring. John Wayne didn't much like his new name but went along with it for professional reasons. He was about to make his first Western.

Image is all important. Comedian Clerow Wilson changed his first name to Flip, which perfectly suits this fast-talking funny man.

Some star names spring from unusual sources. Actor Zero Mostel's first name was taken from his school record. Had he studied harder he might have been known as A Mostel, or at least C+.

Then there are the one-name names like Sonny, Cher, Hildegarde, Twiggy and Ann-Margaret. They sound intimate and have the quick impact of an ad, which they really are.

The route to the right stage name is often meandering. Starlet Phyllis Isley made a number of B-grade movies before becoming Jennifer Jones and winning an Oscar. Bernard Schwartz made his first movies as Jimmie Curtis. Then, remembering his lean childhood years, he decided to try Anthony Adverse. He ended up Tony Curtis.

Popular actress Ellen Burstyn went through a variety of identities and names before she hit paydirt. She appeared on TV as Edna Rae, danced as Keri Flynn, took a screen test as Erica Dean and originally appeared on Broadway as Ellen McRae. This goes to show how close finding a name can lead you to finding yourself.

George Spelvin is a very special stage name. In theatrical tradition, it is the name for an actor who wishes to remain anonymous—because he's playing a second part in the same play, or because the play is so bad he doesn't want to admit he's in it but needs the money. His anonymous sister? Georgina, of course.

Some Superstars and the Real Names They Were Born Under

Lucille Le Sueur = Joan Crawford
Norma Jean Mortenson = Marilyn Monroe
Allen Stewart Konigsberg = Woody Allen
Anna Sofia Cecilia Kalogeropoulos = Maria Callas
Tula Finklea = Cyd Charisse
Rosine Bernhard = Sarah Bernhardt
Greta Louisa Gustafon = Greta Garbo
Benjamin Kubelsky = Jack Benny
Desiderio Alberto Arnaz de Acha III = Desi Arnaz
Natasha Gurdin = Natalie Wood
Rudolpho d'Antonguolla = Rudolph Valentino
Leonard Slye = Roy Rogers
Shirley Schrift = Shelley Winters
Spangler Arlington Brugh = Robert Taylor
Doris Kappelhoff = Doris Day
Archibald Leach = Cary Grant
Steveland Morris Hardaway = Stevie Wonder
Joe Yule, Jr = Mickey Rooney
Sophia Scicolone = Sophia Loren
Vincent Damon Furnier = Alice Cooper
Aaron Chwatt = Red Buttons
Smylla Brind = Vanessa Brown

Chapter Twelve
Pen Names

Pen names are fictitious or made-up names used by writers. They are also called pseudonyms. Why would a writer want a false name? Why not use his real name?

For many reasons: He may have a name that's cumbersome and impossible to remember, like Theodor Jozef Konrad Korzeniowski, who shortened his name to Joseph Conrad. She may be a literary giant, like Pearl Buck, who also wants to write lighter stories, so she writes them under a variety of pen names.

Writers in oppressed countries and politically sticky situations use pen names so they, or their families, won't suffer. O. Henry (real name William Sidney Porter) picked a pen name to conceal his jail record.

In the 17th and 18th centuries when the theatre was looked down upon, prominent men wrote plays under false names such as "A Person of Honour" to protect their reputations.

In the Victorian Era, many women used pen names to conceal their sex. Mary Ann Evans, who wrote as George Eliot, simply found it easier to get published. More recently, novelist Janet Taylor Caldwell wrote under Taylor Caldwell. She felt men would be more likely to read her books if her name sounded masculine.

Today, most women use their real feminine names even when writing about mainly masculine subjects such as football or the stock market. Sylvia Porter, who began writing financial news as S.F. Porter, has switched back to Sylvia—and is increasingly successful. Today, some men acquire feminine pen names, particularly when writing romantic "Gothic" novels.

A number of pen names are shaped for effect. Frank Morrison Spillane used Mickey Spillane to write his hard-hitting detective stories. It sounded rough and tough, like a detective. William Claude Dunkinfield was known as W.C. Fields, which sounded quick and witty, as he was.

Theodore Seuss Geisel carefully chose Dr. Seuss as a pen name for writing children's books. It conveys both a sense of fun and of authority. Another children's book writer, Melville Lyle Boring, had a contest. Object: a more memorable middle name. The winner came up with M. Hardly Boring.

On the other side of the pen name coin, writer Isaac Asimov was told early in his career that no one would buy a book with a name like Isaac Asimov on the cover. He has just successfully published his 200th!

Chapter Thirteen
Criminal and Code Names

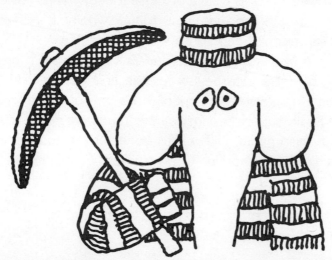

An alias is an assumed name, most often taken by a criminal who doesn't want you to know who he really is. Ex-convicts sometimes use aliases so they can get good jobs and live down bad reputations.

The Justice Department has been known to give legal aliases to someone who might be hounded or hurt if his true identity were known—for instance, someone whose testimony has helped catch a fellow criminal. Sometimes the entire family are given new names, new social security numbers and, thereby, a new start.

The odd thing about aliases is that most people pick a name similar to their real name. In about half the cases the same initials are kept, as Robert Morton chooses alias Richard Moran. Or, the name may be borrowed from a relative or close friend. It is as if the person picking an alias wants to hide who he is, and at the same time keep some sense of identity.

A New York man named Zakar filled out more than 60 false income tax returns and got "refunds" bilking the government out of thousands of dollars. He was finally caught because all the fraudulent names he chose also began with Z. His constant Z acted like a flag alerting authorities to his true identity.

Code Names

A code name is something else. Such a name is used to conceal the person's identity for security (not crimi nal) reasons. Government code names are used for security, especially during war time. They are zip quick and easy to say. During World War 11, President Roosevelt's code name was Admiral Q; General Eisenhower's was Duckpin.

Road Handles

CB handles are a new light-hearted kind of alias. CB handles are the fanciful names truckers and owners of citizen band radios use when they talk to each other on the road.

They are oddball names that bear little relation to their owner's real name—names like Hog Caller, Gutsy Bert and Spitfire. President Ford's wife Betty took the handle, First Mama. A perfect example, it is brief, breezy and good-humored. It says something about the kind of person she is.

Winnie Ruth Judd was an infamous woman criminal who hacked up a number of her friends. Forty years after her conviction she changed her name to Marion Lane.

As Winnie Ruth Judd, she was hard and heartless, a real tiger woman. As Marion Lane, she became compassionate and a contributing member of society. She ended her days peacefully working in a home for the elderly. The name change literally changed her life.

Chapter Fourteen
Humorous Handles

Zazu Zilch, Newton Hooten, Hugh Pugh, and Xerces Yuki are funny (real) names because they sound funny.

Etta Apple, Mack Aroni, Jack Ash and Cigar Stubbs are funny because they make words. Buncha Love, Nita Bath and Justin Tune go a step further.

There is a Katz Meow, a Pinchas Katz and a Katz Cradle, as well as a company named Katz Pajamas. The country is full of Peter Rabbits, Angel Devines and June Moons. Warren Peach and Basil Reader represent the literary side of names.

The most famous humorous handles belong to a Texas sister and brother, Ima Hogg and Yura Hogg. Both grew up to be prominent people and were well-rounded and happy in spite of (or because of?) their names.

In New York, there is an Ah Sze Yu. In Money, Mississippi, there is a Penny Nichols.

Initials enhance the humor of some names such as A. Clampit, B. Goode, T. Hee, O. Hell, R.U. High and U. Nutt. In the Virgin Islands, a commissioner of education was named A. Moron.

Names and occupations often enhance each other. There are numerous doctors with the last name of Doctor, and even a Doctor Doctor. There are also Butchers and Bonebreakers who are doctors.

There is a nurse named Rose Blood, a psychiatrist named Yuri Strange, a science reporter named Storm Field, an undertaker named Groaner Digger and a business advisor named Manly Cheit. A man named Roy Takencarof was, it figures, a jail keeper.

People also write books that reflect their names. Henry Still is the author of IN QUEST OF QUIET. Elizabeth Sprigge wrote THE LIFE OF IVY COMPTON-BURNETT and Mary Brested is responsible for OH! SEX EDUCATION. A Reckless writes about criminology, a Kamell about the Middle East, and a man named Smellie specializes in chemical reactivity.

Some names even act as self-fulfilling prophesies. Charles Flesh and Chic Blood worked together in an airlines office. The two people involved in a 1959 car accident were a Mr. Crash and a Miss Collision. And a woman named Mrs. L. E. Fant has an outstanding collection of guess what.

The Way They Answer the Phone

A man named Central Still used to answer his phone, "Hello, this is Central Still speaking."

A Joseph F. St. Peter, who was a morgue attendant, answered his with, "The morgue, St. Peter speaking."